Eat... aNd Eat... aNd Eat...

Chicago's ethnic neighbourhoods are great places to try foods from all over the world! True Italian pasta, Swedish köttbullar (meatballs) and Mexican quesadillas are just a few examples. There are thousands of restaurants (7,000-plus, to be more exact) in the city. And, of course, no trip to Chicago would be complete without a visit to a pizzeria for a 'Chicago-style' deep-dish pizza. Yummy. The crust of this pizza can be an inch thick, maybe more!

caTcH a RidE oN tHE L oR tHE mEtRa

You can get to most attractions in the Loop and surrounding areas by train—the 'L'. If you want to go somewhere farther from the city centre, try the Metra. Visit www.transitchicago.com or www.metrarail.com for more information. And to make getting around even easier, check out the interactive transit map online:

http://maps.google.com/help/maps/transit/chicago

gEt REady foR youR visit!!!

For more information, visit the City of Chicago's Official Tourism site (www.explorechicago.org) and download cool audio tours. They've even got one just for kids! The Chicago Convention & Tourism Bureau's website (www.choosechicago.com) is also full of information. Or drop by the Visitor Information Center at the Chicago Cultural Center, 77 East Randolph Street.

Make sure you pick up the Go Chicago Card (check www.gochicagocard.com) or the Chicago City Pass (check www.citypass.com/city/chicago.html) to get cheaper tickets— and sometimes even get in free—to lots of Chicago sights!

If you have any tips or questions for Junior Jetsetters, email us at: **FEEDBACK@JUNIORJETSETTERS.COM**

Between 1870 and 1900, the city's growth attracted new people from rural areas and from Europe, causing it to become the fastest-growing city in the world at the time. This rush of immigrants is still reflected in the multicultural neighbourhoods of Chicago.

tHE L-tRaiN caME to towN

In 1893, the World's Columbian Exposition attracted over 25 million visitors to Chicago. The fair celebrated the 400th anniversary of Christopher Columbus's landing in America. The 'Alley L,' an elevated train, was introduced to provide transportation to the fair. And it's still there! Make sure to try it while you're in town, and wave at some of the people working in the offices as you ride by.

chicaGo got a bit of a bad REp

During the 1920s, Chicago gained a reputation as a lawless city. Gangsters thrived in major cities like Chicago, where they could sell alcohol during Prohibition (a time when alcohol was banned). The most famous of these gangsters was Al Capone.

chicaGo today:
EXpERiENcE tHE oH-so EtHNic city

Chicago is made up of many different neighbourhoods, each with its own unique history, people and architecture. These include the Loop, Lincoln Park, Hyde Park and Pilsen, just to name a few.

Some areas are associated with ethnic groups, such as Andersonville (Swedes), Pilsen & Little Village (Mexicans) and Near West Side (Italians & Greeks). Don't be surprised to hear different languages when you visit neighbourhoods in and around downtown.

trader. He built his settlement in 1779 at the mouth of the Chicago River and married a Potawatomi native woman. He left in 1800, but is still considered "The Father of Chicago."

cHicaGo GREw, aNd GREw, aNd GREw

The Town of Chicago was incorporated in 1833 with a population of 350. The population grew quickly and in 1837, with 4,170 residents, it was officially made a city. The Illinois and Michigan Canal, which connected Chicago with the Mississippi River, was completed in 1848. This, along with the arrival of the first locomotive, helped the city to become a major transportation hub. By 1857, more than 90,000 people called Chicago home!

tHERE was a biG fiRE

On October 8, 1871, The Great Chicago fire started on the west side of the city. It lasted two days, claimed 300 lives, left 90,000 people homeless and destroyed $200 million worth of property. An early report claimed that the fire started when a cow kicked over a lantern in a barn, but the story was later found to be false. Really, nobody knows what caused the fire, but the rumour just won't go away. Most people still blame the cow!

a biGGER, bEttER city was REboRN

The Great Chicago Fire was tragic, but it did create an opportunity to plan and rebuild the city. During the reconstruction, only the newest materials and methods were used, and the result was a city that rivalled New York. Chicago became known as the birthplace of modern architecture.

what do you KNOw about chicaGo?

Chicago is known for its great buildings; amazing pizza; ethnic neighbourhoods; and beautiful waterfront… not to mention its baseball team, the Chicago Cubs. It's the third most populated city in North America and it's the financial, industrial and cultural centre of the Midwest. The city's metropolitan area covers parts of the states of Illinois, Wisconsin and Indiana, around the southwest shore of Lake Michigan.

How cool is that?

Chicago, a.k.a. Windy City, Second City, Chi-Town and City of Broad Shoulders, has a lot of cool things going for it. The first skyscraper was built there in the late 19th century. It seemed huge at the time, but the Home Insurance Building wouldn't even count as a skyscraper today. (It was only 10 storeys high!) The world's largest indoor aquarium is in Chicago. And check this out: there are more green roofs there than in any other North American city. Coolest of all, though, is the Chicago River. It's the only river in the world that flows backwards. Engineers actually reversed its course!!

a littlE histoRy: tHE fiRst sEttlERs sEttlEd iN

The first people to live in Chicago were Native Americans, mostly Algonquian Peoples. They included the Miamis, Potawatomis and Illinois native groups. In fact the name 'Chicago' is the French translation of 'shikaakwa,' the Miami-Illinois word for 'wild leek' or 'skunk.' In the late 1600s, the area was visited by French explorers. The first non-Native American settler was Jean Baptiste Pointe du Sable, a Haitian fur

activitiES iN amStERdam

out-of-toWN aNd FuRtHER afiEld

youR list of stuff to sEE aNd do

Junior Jetsetters™ Guide to Chicago
First edition February 2009
ISBN-13: 978-0-9784601-1-2

Published in Toronto by Junior Jetsetters Inc.
3044 Bloor St. W., Suite 550, Toronto, ON M8X 2Y8 (Canada)
Text: Pedro F. Marcelino, Slawko Waschuk
Sub-Editor: Anna Humphrey
Characters: Mike Hiscott
Illustrations: Brian Ayers, Briggen Baity, Joshua Boyle, Alyssa Colyette, David
Finkelstein, Israel Franco, David Gueringer, David Kingly, DeAndre Knight,
Isaac Mack, Eben Mazzeri, Alaine Ross, coordinated locally by Yesica Barrera
and Claudia Bernardette (After School Matters, City of Chicago)
Cover Design: Pedro F. Marcelino, set in Casual Font by A.J. Palmer
Cover Art: David Finkelstein, Tapan Gandhi (logo), Kim Sokol (stamp)

Special Thanks to: Karen Ryan, Juliette Price, Viola Lee (City of Chicago),
Sheridan College Institute of Technology, Hilton Suites, Chicago's Essex Inn

Library and Archives Canada Cataloguing in Publication

Marcelino, Pedro F., 1978-
     Junior Jetsetters guide to Chicago / Pedro F. Marcelino, Slawko
Waschuk ; edited by Anna Humphrey ; illustrated by John Michael
Hiscott, Tapan Gandhi and students of the After School Matters of the
City of Chicago.

ISBN 978-0-9784601-1-2

     1. Chicago (Ill.)--Guidebooks--Juvenile literature.
I. Waschuk, Slawko, 1974- II. Humphrey, Anna, 1979- III. Hiscott, John
Michael, 1986- IV. Gandhi, Tapan, 1986- V. Title. VI. Title: Guide to
Chicago.

F548.18.M37 2009   j917.73'110444   C2008-907852-7

Printed and bound in China by Everbest Printing Co Ltd.

JUNIOR Jetsetters™ guide to

CHICAGO

In cooperation with

after school matters

After School Matters is a non-profit organization that offers Chicago teens innovative out-of-school activities through science37, sports37, tech37 words37 and the nationally recognized gallery37 programs. These programs are provided through a network of public and private partnerships that include the City of Chicago, Chicago Public Schools, Chicago Park District, Chicago Public Library and community-based organizations. The hands-on programs expose teens to rewarding careers and help them to develop marketable job skills. After School Matters students have illustrated several of the Chicago attractions featured in this book. For more information, visit:
www.afterschoolmatters.org

map of the city center,
the loop and Navy Pier

pERfEct pRaiRiE stylE dEsiGNs

Since we're talking architecture, no visit to Chicago is complete without a visit to Frederick C. Robie House, one of the last homes that Frank Lloyd Wright designed while he lived in Oak Park. It's also one of the most important buildings in the history of American architecture! This is because it's a perfect example of a Prairie Style house (a house done in the style that Wright was most famous for).

The Robie House was built in 1910 and was owned by different families until 1926. After that, it became a dorm for many years until it was finally donated to the University of Chicago, who opened it to the public. How do you think 'Prairie style' got its name? Is there anything about the Robie house that reminds you of the prairies?

Back in Oak Park, you'll find the Unity Temple. In 1905, Unity Church's steeple was struck by lightning and the building burned down. In its place, Unity Temple was built. Frank Lloyd Wright designed it while living in Oak Park. The temple has two separate areas: the temple space and a community/meeting space. It's the only public building that still exists from Wright's Prairie style period.

a WHOlE NEW viEw of tHE city

It's not really surprising that Chicago—the city that invented the skyscraper—has the tallest one in North America. It was even the tallest in the world until the Petronas Twin Towers were built in 1998 in Kuala Lumpur, Malaysia (but if you count the antennas, it's still the highest).

The Sears Tower was built in 1970, when executives from Sears, Roebuck & Co. (a Chicago retailer) decided to put up a building that could accommodate all of their many employees under one roof. It took 110 storeys of office space, but they got them all in! The building would have been even taller, too, if it wasn't for the fact that the Federal Aviation Administration told them to stop. They were worried that, if it got any higher, airplanes and helicopters might accidentally run into it! The building isn't owned by Sears these days, but the name hasn't changed.

There are 104 elevators to chose from when you visit, but you should perhaps catch a ride on one of the 16 double-deckers. Be sure to make it all the way to the Skydeck on the 103rd floor—412 metres (1,353 feet) up. The view, which is amazing, isn't the only thing to see up there! There's also a cool exhibit about the history of Chicago!

cool, yEah?

At 527 metres (1,729 feet), Sears Tower is the tallest in the US, but not in the world, because its antennas are not part of the structure. Taiwan's Taipei 101 as well as Malaysia's Petronas Towers are taller, but Dubai's Burj Dubai will soon rise above them all!

GEt caUGHt Up iN jEWiSH CultuRE

Come and explore Jewish culture at the Spertus Institute. The institute, which opened in 1924 as the College of Jewish Studies, is an organization open to everyone and is not associated with any specific Jewish group. Its focus is on learning and on encouraging everyone to explore what it means to be Jewish. There's a museum, a library and a college as well as a collection of historic and antique items, and a changing exhibit that addresses current culture.

There's also a place just for kids: the Gray Children's Center. When you visit, you can learn about Hebrew letters and language, or listen to traditional Jewish stories and create new ones yourself. Did you know Hebrew, unlike English, is written from right to left? Do you know how it sounds? Come find out!

cool, yEaH?

The Hebrew alphabet (called alefbet) has no vowels, only consonants.

In North America, many Jews speak Yiddish, which is a linguistic mix of Hebrew and medieval German. In Yiddish, the alphabet is called Alef-Beyz.

68

SEE a cubs' HomE Run and gRab a HotdoG too!

What do baseball, fast food and chewing gum have in common? They all helped bring baseball to the city of Chicago! Major League baseball started in 1876, and the American League was created in 1901. However, in 1912, a new league was formed to compete with the Major League. It was called the Federal League. In 1914, Charlie Weeghman (a businessman who gained his fortune by starting fast-food restaurants in Chicago) built a park for his Federal League baseball team, the Chicago Federals. The park was called Weeghman Park. After only two years, though, the Federal League disappeared. Weeghman got together with William Wrigley, Jr. (the owner of Wrigley's chewing gum) and several other men to buy the Cubs, a team from the National League. After a few years, Wrigley bought the team from the other owners and renamed the park Cubs Park. In 1926, it was renamed Wrigley Field.

Whether you like baseball or not, the Chicago Cubs are the soul of Chicago. If you have a chance, go and watch them in their home turf, and hang out with some passionate Chicagoans enjoying their innings!

cool, yEaH?

The centre field scoreboard has never been hit by a home run, but it has been hit by a golf ball!

Some of the houses around the park have official seats on their roofs so that additional fans can watch the games!

tHE WHOlE woRld iN cHicaGo‼

Chicago is a very multicultural city. It makes sense, then, that there are tons of museums that celebrate the culture, art and history of the different people who live here.

Swedes were once one of the largest ethnic groups in Chicago. Their biggest community was located in the Andersonville neighbourhood on the north side. Even though the area no longer has a huge number of Swedes, it's still strongly associated with Swedish culture and it's the location of the **Swedish American Museum Center**. The museum, which started as a small one-room log cabin, aims to display and promote Swedish art, history and culture. The permanent exhibit, The Dream of America— Swedish Immigration to Chicago, is all about what it was like for Swedish people to immigrate to the city. The Children's Museum of Immigration is a hands-on, touch-everything-you-see museum that tells you their story and lets you get in their skin (quite literally!).

Chicago has the world's biggest Polish population outside of Warsaw, the capital of Poland! There were three main waves of migration. The first lasted until 1920, the second wave happened after World War II and the third wave was in the 1980s. Polish people came to Chicago from different areas for different reasons. Some were poor farmers, others were professionals, writers and artists. This had a huge impact on Polish culture and communities across the city. Polish Catholic parishes, schools, organizations and businesses grew with the population. Major Polish newspapers even opened offices in the city! The **Polish Museum of America**, in the historic Polish Downtown in West Town, celebrates their history, culture and art (folk costumes, sculptures and wooden carvings).

Africans and African-Americans have a long history in Chicago. The first non-native settler in the area was Jean Baptiste Pointe du Sable, a Haitian fur trader of African and French descent. Over the years, much of the African-American population that came to Chicago arrived from the south. Chicago was then the 'capital of black America,' with very influential and prominent black individuals, as well as the most widely read black newspaper in the US. The Great Migration, which had two waves, increased Chicago's African-American population from 2 percent to 33 percent! And with the people came their culture. Jazz and Blues music (SEE PaGE 88), for instance, was brought to the city during this time. Links to the south, and especially to Mississippi, were so strong that the south is still considered 'home' for many black Chicagoans. **The DuSable Museum of African American History** highlights the experiences of African-Americans, their achievements and history.

Just outside Chicago, you'll find one of the few museums that focuses on the Native people of North America. Its main exhibits showcase the native cultures of the American Woodlands, Plains, Southwest, Northwest Coast and Arctic peoples. The Chicago area was once home to Woodland Natives, such as the Miami, the Sauk, the Fox, or most recently the Potawatomi bands. The first houses in the Chicago area were long houses and wigwams (a half-size version is located in the museum)— nothing like the wood and brick structures that the non-native settlers built later. The **Mitchell Museum of the American Indian** has 'touching tables' in each gallery where kids can touch real items, like pottery, beadwork, clothing, tools, snakeskin and buffalo fur!

tHE placE a GiRl's doll GoEs to SHop aNd GEt pampEREd

If you like dolls, American Girl Place is going to seem like heaven on earth! The store sells a line of dolls and accessories based on pre-teen-girl characters from various periods of American history. Each doll comes with a book about her adventures. You can also pick up some furniture for your new friend, not to mention clothes, shoes and more. She can even have her own pet, if she wants one! Or, why not shop for a doll from the Just Like You series. You can choose from a huge variety of dolls to find one that shares both your looks and your personality, then take her on a shopping spree!

Since the American Girl company opened in 1986, it's been focused on celebrating the potential of girls ages 3 to 12. American Girl encourages girls to dream, to grow, to aspire, to create, and to imagine. Visit the store and plan to spend a whole afternoon, not only shopping, but also hanging out having tea with your dolls in the doll café, getting your portrait taken at the photo studio, or watching your doll get pampered at the hair salon.

cool, yEah?

*The American Girl Place website
(www.americangirl.com) has lots of online
games you can play. There's also a magazine full of
tips and activities that you can subscribe to!*

*If your doll is sick, bring it to the doll clinic at
American Girl Place. A doll doctor will help her out!*

it StaRts with thREE bald Guys painted bluE...thEN GEts wEiRd

When you go to see the Blue Man Group, be prepared to be amazed. It's a long, long way from your average show! The show features three performers with blue-painted faces, called Blue Men. They don't speak, but they do play a mixture of instruments unlike any you've ever seen before... that is, unless you happen to be familiar with the tubulum, the airpoles, the drumbone, the drumulum, the dogulum or the piano smasher.

During the show, the Blue Men also use mime, props, audience members, lighting, and lots and lots of paper to entertain you with fabulous antics. You'll also be amazed to see what they can do with marshmallows. And if you don't get grossed out easily, try getting a seat near the front, in the 'poncho section.' Just be warned, you will get wet! (Good luck convincing your parents to sit here!) Don't be late though, or you might become part of the show. For real. Don't believe us? Give it a try and you'll see!

cool, yEaH?

The group has developed two musical instruments for kids—Keyboard Experience and Percussion Tubes, made by Toy Quest. Are you feeling Blue?

cool, yEah?

The Tribune Tower contains bricks and stones from a lot of famous buildings all over the world: the Taj Mahal (India), the Great Wall of China (China), the Great Pyramid (Egypt), the Parthenon (Greece), Notre Dame de Paris (France), Hagia Sophia (Turkey), the Palace of Westminster (Great Britain), the Berlin Wall (Germany) and even the White House!

Sail doWN tHE RivERsidE foR a GREat viEw of cHicaGo

One of the best ways to see Chicago's amazing architecture is by boat. On an architecture boat tour, you'll cruise the Chicago River past 50-or-so important and historic buildings, and you will also get a unique perspective on the city as a whole.

Check out the Equitable Building near the lake, which is believed to be the original site of Jean Baptiste Pointe duSable's cabin (therefore, the 'beginning of Chicago')! Marina City, which looks like two ears of corn, is a self-contained complex with residences, offices, shops, entertainment facilities and its own boat-garage (it has appeared in a lot of movies!). The Merchandise Mart is the second largest building in the US, right after the Pentagon, and it even has its very own zip code! Look up when you go under the bridges and, if you're lucky, you'll see one being raised. Chicago has more moving bridges than any city in the world, including Amsterdam. These architecture boat tours are organized by several different companies, including the Chicago Architecture Foundation (CAF), the Chicago History Museum, ShoreLine Sightseeing, Wendella Boats and Seadog.

calling all junior filmmakers!

Chicago has a film festival just for kids and, when you take part in it, you'll have the chance to be much more than an audience member. Some of the films are produced by kids themselves, and films are judged by separate juries of children and adults!

In addition to the annual festival, Facets (the organization that runs the festival) offers film classes for kids, where you can learn what it takes to create a film from scratch (writing, producing, filming and more) and then you actually get to do it! Or if you're more into watching movies, learn how to critique films and write reviews about them. If you love cartoons, work with animators to create short, animated films. You'll have the chance to come up with stories, create animated characters, storyboards and backgrounds and use an animation camera to put it all together. And if you're already a junior filmmaker, why not submit your movie to the festival for a chance to have it shown? How cool would that be?

cool, yeah?

Each year, over 200 films from more than 40 countries are shown during the Chicago International Children's Film Festival. Also keep in mind that films shown in the competition program of the CICFF can also qualify for Academy Awards (which you might now as Oscars... yes, THOSE Oscars)!

COME lEaRN tHE RopES fROM REal tRapEZE pRos

Have you ever wondered what it takes to be in the circus? Here's your chance to find out! At the Flying Gaonas Trapeze School, you'll learn the ropes of the flying trapeze (literally) from seventh generation performers who have been in the circus business since they were kids. There are actually many kinds of trapeze, but the flying trapeze is one of the best known. It's where the performers grab trapeze bars, swing in the air and then release them in time for other performers to catch them, all high above the ground.

At the Flying Gaonas Gym, you'll learn the basics, like how to take off and swing, then move on to perform some tricks. And just tell your parents not to worry! There's a net below and harnesses attached to the rigging, for extra safety!

cool, yEaн?

The flying trapeze was invented by Jules Léotard in France in the late 1800s. He also invented leotards, the colourful skin-tight outfits that gymnasts and trapeze artists commonly wear.

Julio Gaona, one of the gym's founders began his career at the age of three performing on the trampoline for Circus Gatti with his father, brother and sister.

80

cool, yEaH?

Al Capone wasn't arrested for racketeering (running illegal businesses), but for not paying his taxes! It was the only way the authorities could find to get him in jail.

a tRip to cHicaGo's sHady past

You can join a Gangster Tour and enjoy a journey into the past as you cruise the streets of Chicago in search of old hangouts like the Lexington Hotel, gambling dens and shootout sites! In the 1920s, Chicago was famous (or maybe we should say infamous) for bootlegging— making, selling and transporting alcohol. Alcohol was banned in 1919 by the 18th Amendment. It was a very unpopular law across the country and demand for alcohol continued, which caused organized crime to grow as gangsters supplied the now illegal drink.

There were gangsters in all major cities then, but the most famous of them lived in Chicago. His name was Alphonse Gabriel Capone, or Al Capone. He controlled speakeasies (places that sold alcohol), gambling houses, horse and racetracks, nightclubs, distilleries and breweries. It's been said that he made over $100 million a year from 1925–1930. He avoided arrest by bribing the police, judges, prosecutors and important Chicago politicians. But, in 1931, the law finally caught up with him. He spent about seven years in prison, most of that time in the escape-proof island prison of Alcatraz, in San Francisco. Two years after his arrest, the 21st Amendment repealed (or cancelled out) the 18th Amendment, making alcohol legal again. It was the only amendment to ever be repealed.

tAKE iN SOME tuNES outdooRS

The Jay Pritzker Pavilion is one of the key features of Millennium Park (SEE PaGE 20). It's an outdoor concert hall, but it's not just a performance space—like most buildings created by its mega-famous architect, a Canadian man called Frank O. Gehry, it's a work of art, too! It looks more like a giant ancient samurai headdress than a stage!

Every year at the pavilion you can attend the Grant Park Music Festival, an outdoor classical music series (the only free one in the country). The festival has been going on since 1935 and was started to make classical music available to all Chicagoans. Today it is enjoyed by residents and visitors alike. The main performers are the Grant Park Orchestra and the Grant Park Chorus, but classical music isn't the only kind of music you can hear. You can listen to jazz during the Made in Chicago: World Class Jazz series or world music during the World Music Festival. Occasionally, dance performances can also be seen here. And in the summer, if you stop by in the afternoon, you might catch performances by singers, storytellers and entertainers or hear the Grant Park Orchestra and Chorus rehearsing.

cool, yEah?

The pavilion was built in such a way that any of the 12,000 people sitting in the huge lawn will feel like they're in the front row!

The pavilion stands 36 metres (120 feet) high, to the tip of the tallest piece of metal.

take a NicE, slow cRuisE oR dash past tHE wavEs iN a spEEdboat

Chicago's skyline is one of the most impressive in the United States, and thanks to the Sears Tower, the John Hancock and the Smurfit-Stone buildings, it's also one of the most recognizable (SEE tHE skyliNE oN paGE 14). Some of the best views of the city are actually from the water though! Several companies have lake cruises that travel up and down the Lake Michigan coast, most leaving from Navy Pier. A visit to the pier isn't complete until you hop on one of these cruises and battle the Lake Michigan waves. Relax and take in the sights, or choose a cruise that tells you a brief history of the city (which, by now, you aldredy know a bit about). The best times to go are early in the morning or close to sunset, especially in the summer, when it's really warm.

For further history, some cruises head inland onto the Chicago River. (Or you can pick a specialized river cruise - SEE paGE 76). If what you like is speed, you'll have to hop aboard one of the sunflower-yellow speedboats at Navy Pier. You'll race up the coast like you're in an action movie boat chase! But be warned, you **will** get (very) wet!

cool, yEah?

Lake Michigan used to be really polluted, but the many states that surround it (and the City of Chicago itself) cleaned it up big time—it's so clean now that the water looks like you could be down in the Caribbean!!

The yellow Seadog speedboats have some serious power, with turbo-charged 1,000 horsepower engines!

CatcH tHE gRoovE aNd SWiNG aloNG 'SWEEt HoMe cHicaGo'!

If you've got the blues, you've come to the right place. In the 1920s, after jazz and blues music spread from the south, Chicago became America's jazz and blues music hub. 'The Stroll'—the section of State Street between 31st and 39th streets on the south side—was where you could hear things like the boogie-woogie. Many well-known jazz artists like Louis Armstrong, Earl Hines and Jelly Roll Morton were showcased in Chicago. Benny Goodman, 'the King of Swing' was originally from Chicago. It wasn't long before clubs started to open up in the Loop district. The Green Mill is one of the city's oldest jazz clubs and is still around after all this time.

'Sweet Home Chicago,' as the city was often called, was also known for its blues clubs, mostly in the city's south side. Some were really small—only a counter for a bar and a few tables. One popular club, called Pepper's, was so small that only three musicians could perform at one time! Well-known clubs featured artists like Big Bill Broonzy, Little Walter, Otis Spann and Muddy Waters. The House of Blues and Blue Chicago are the most famous blues clubs in the city today.

cool, yEaH?

Blues was born in the Mississippi Delta and was brought to Chicago by Afro-Americans during the Great Migration.

One of Al Capone's men owned 25% of the Green Mill jazz club during the 1920s.

sHop till you dRop!!!

There are nearly 500 shops in the small eight-block area called the Magnificent Mile, so if you're a shop-a-holic, be sure to set aside a whole day (and lots of cash)! Stores include American Girl Place, the Disney Store, LEGO Global Family Attractions, ESPN Zone, Niketown and Hershey's Chicago. There are also 200 restaurants and over 50 hotels! And shopping isn't the only thing to do! Check out some of the seasonal events like the Magnificent Mile Lights Festival in the fall, TOAST on The Magnificent Mile (where adults can sample different champagnes) and Fireworks Spectacular in the winter, Tulip Days in the spring and Gardens of Chicago's Magnificent Mile in the summer.

Back in the 1920s, when it was first constructed, the Magnificent Mile (or North Michigan Avenue, its actual name) was the most prominent and prestigious area in Chicago, and today it's still the top street in the city, and one of the top streets in the world. As you walk and shop, see if you can pick out some buildings in the styles Chicago is famous for: Beaux-Arts, Gothic revival and modern.

cool, yEah?

The Champs-Élysées in Paris was the inspiration for the Magnificent Mile.

Chicago's slogan "Mile After Magnificent Mile" is based on this shopping area.

91

do a doublE aXEl oR laNd flaT oN youR facE

If you're in Chicago during the winter months, lace up your skates like every Chicagoan out there and head to McCormick Tribune Ice Rink, right in the middle of Millennium Park (SEE paGE 20)! You'll feel like a pro as you do your spins, lifts, toe jumps and triple axels! But if you don't know how to skate on ice, don't worry: you're not the only one. Just give it a try and, if you fall, remember that the most important thing is to keep your hands off the ice all the time!!!! (You really don't want anyone to skate right through them.)

The McCormick Tribune Plaza is one of about 10 rinks open in Chicago each winter. Music plays while people are skating, particularly Christmas music during the holidays, and it's one of the most popular places in the city to people watch. If the rink looks familiar to you, it's probably because you've seen it before in Hollywood movies filmed in Chicago! Since it's an outdoor rink, there's no skating in the summer months, but there are often exhibits in the same space, and right behind it you can rest for a few minutes at the beautiful peristyle (the huge half-moon porch with pillars).

cool, yEaH?

The ice rink was the first feature of Millennium Park to open to the public, in 2001.

It is larger than the Rockefeller Center ice rink in New York City.

EXPERiENCE diffERENt cultuREs withOut lEaViNG thE city

Chicago's population boomed over the years as millions of people from Europe and other parts of the world came to live in the city. As a result, dozens of unique neighbourhoods sprang up (chEck out a complEtE map oN pagE 7). Chicago's neighbourhood tours are a great way to learn about different ethnic groups. In fact, it's the famous friendliness of Chicagoans and the easygoing feel in Chicago's neighbourhoods that helped build the city's great reputation in the first place! Today, there are about 210 of these neighbourhoods, and it's sometimes hard to tell where one stops and another begins! The city has recently defined 77 community areas so that things are less confusing.

Each neighbourhood has a unique identity based on its people, its history, its architecture and its culture. As you walk through each neighbourhood, look at the local shops and restaurants: what do they sell? What is written on the signs? Can you read them? Try to notice the different atmospheres in the streets. Different neighbourhoods can sometimes look like completely different cities, even when they're right beside each other!

cool, yEaH?

Chicago is home to the world's largest Polish population outside of Warsaw, the capital of Poland!

Some of the neighbourhoods got their names from the original residents, but in many cases they have been replaced by newcomers from other countries.

96

MEET THE STARS OF THE STABLE

The horses that live and perform at Chicago's Noble Horse Theatre come from all over the world and are chosen for their unique talents and abilities. They're trained in classical riding, which involves some pretty fancy footwork. The performances you can see at the theatre display this type of riding and include moves such as pas de deux, carriage acts, quadrilles, liberty acts and airs above ground. The theatre also features Cossack riding (primarily Russian stunt riding), which is considered both a sport and a martial art (a martial art is a sport that was once used as training for war). The horses and their riders put on different shows depending on the time of year. As Hallowe'en nears, they do *The Legend of Sleepy Hollow* (which might creep you out), and during the holidays, it's *The Nutcracker*.

The building itself dates back to 1871, right after the Great Chicago Fire. At that time, it was a riding hall (it's now the last one still standing). It held up to 60 horses, some of which were used for pulling coaches and carriages. In the 1920s, the building became a riding school, and in 2000 it gained its current form.

cool, yEah?

The horses that pull the beautiful white carriages on Michigan Avenue are stabled in this barn.

Quadrilles, like those you'll see at the Noble Horse Theatre, are formations of even numbers of horses (originally four) performing in square-shaped figures.

youR aNtiquE RidE iS oN fiRE!

Ride through the streets in an antique fire truck as you learn about the history of the Great Chicago Fire of 1871. It was one of the biggest disasters in 19th century America. During the fire, about four square miles burnt down and hundreds of people died. The fire department was completely unprepared, their equipment wasn't good enough and they didn't have enough men. The fire started in a small shed on DeKoven Street. It was first blamed on a cow kicking over a lantern and setting a barn on fire (but this was later proven false, and the poor cow was acquitted).

After the blaze, the city started to rebuild almost immediately. So, while the fire was a disaster, it was also a chance to re-plan the city from scratch. They used only the latest materials and building techniques and, because of this, Chicago became one of the most advanced cities in the United States. Within one year most signs of the fire were gone. The city's fire codes and equipment were improved, and so were building techniques. Before the fire, roads and houses were made of wood. After the fire, houses were built of non-flammable materials like brick, and roads were asphalted. Other cities noticed these changes and followed Chicago's lead. This tour will take you through some of the areas that have been re-developed after the fire and tell you all about what it was like back then.

cool, yEah?

The Old Water Tower is the only public building that survived the fire. It's still standing today.

The second star in the Chicago city flag symbolizes the Great Fire.

a MuSEuM ouT iN tHE StREEtS

As you stroll through the streets of Chicago, be on the lookout for the many sculptures on display. You'll find them mostly in parks and near city-owned buildings. The first outdoor sculpture to be displayed in the city was "The Picasso," by Pablo Picasso. This led to huge interest from the public and sculptures started popping up all over the city, creating a real outdoor museum that people love.

These sculptures became such an important feature of Chicago that the city wanted to continue the tradition. Officials passed a law saying that when buildings owned and operated by the city were built or renovated, they had to contribute to buying more works of street art. The law also stated at least half of this art had to be created by artists from the Chicago area. Today, for just this reason, you can spot more than 100 works of street art as you wander around the city. Most of the sculptures can be found in the Loop. If you want to find out more about the works of art you're seeing, be sure to pick up a Public Art Guide from the Chicago Cultural Center! One of the most recognizable is Jean Dubuffet's sculpture in front of Thompson Plaza.

cool, yEah?

Chicago's public art program is so successful that over 200 cities in the United States have copied it.

Pablo Picasso was offered $100,000 for his work, but he refused it. His sculpture was a gift to Chicago.

MaKE a MiGHty SplaSH

Who doesn't love water slides? Chicago's indoor and outdoor water parks are fun for the whole family. They're great places to take a break from your busy museum and neighbourhood schedule and stop by to make a big splash!

Coco Key Water Resort looks and feels like an island resort, except it's inside! There's something for everyone. If you like going fast, try the Coconut Grove Adventure River tube ride. Other quick-moving waterslides include the Shark Slam, Gator Gush, Barracuda Blast and Pelican Plunge. If you're into sports, then spend some time in the Coral Reef Cavern, an activity pool where you can play water basketball. Or if slow and relaxing is more your speed, check out the Dip-In Theater where you can enjoy videos while floating around in a tube. After a day in the water, you might want to move onto dry land and visit the resort's Key Quest Arcade, which is full of interactive, state-of-the-art video games.

Mayan Adventure Indoor Waterpark's fast-moving water rides include the Grand Mayan Falls tube slide and the Howling Monkey body slide. For something a bit calmer, hop on a tube and make your way down the Oogaboo Lazy River, or get your team together for a game of water basketball in the Twisted Lizard Family Activity pool. And if you don't quite feel like taking the plunge into the pools, check out Parrot Island, an interactive zero-depth playstation. But don't be fooled—the 1,100 litre (300 gallon) dumping bucket is sure to get you wet anyway! But, if you are in the Mayan Waterpark, you probably want to get wet...

Pelican Harbor Indoor/Outdoor Aquatic Park has things to do both inside and outside: pools, waterslides, tube rides, and even a 'river' where you can float away. Outside, you'll also find a sand playground and a beach volleyball pitch. After a fun day, remember to enjoy a quiet picnic to replace some calories and get your energy back on track!

cool, yEaн?

Coco Key's Adventure River is longer than a football field.

Don't like getting cold? Temperatures at the Mayan Adventure Indoor Waterpark are always tropical, a balmy 28°C (82°F).

Catch a horse race or just horse around a bit

Giddy-up and get yourself to Arlington Park if horses are your thing. Aside from watching one of the many horse races, there's plenty else to do. Sundays are family days when the park offers pony rides, a petting zoo, face-painting and special meals for kids. You can even become a member of the Junior Jockey Club to try cool, hands-on activities and learn all about horses and Arlington Park. Each Sunday, you'll try something new, like caring for horses, making derby hats, meeting with jockeys and veterinarians, and all sorts of other equestrian activities. With space for 2,000 horses, there will always be plenty to do!

Horse racing has been popular in Chicago since the 1830s. And, in the 1920s, a time when gangsters like Al Capone had a bad reputation in Chicago, betting on horse races was big business. Arlington Racetrack opened in 1927 after the state of Illinois legalized parimutuel betting (a betting system often used for horse racing). To prevent the city's gangsters from taking over the races, a prominent businessman took control of Arlington Park. The Great Depression and World War II followed, but the track somehow survived, only closing briefly during the war. In 1985, a fire destroyed the original facility but it was rebuilt and re-opened in glory a few years later.

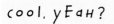
cool, yEah?

Arlington Park was the site of the world's first million dollar race, the Arlington Million.

9 iSlaNds, 155 HEctaREs... aNd a WHolE lot of plaNts!

When Chicago officially became a city in 1837, the motto 'Urbs in Horto' was included in the city's official seal. 'Urbs in Horto' is Latin for 'city in a garden.' It was this motto that inspired the creation of the Chicago Horticultural Society in 1890. And it was this society that went on to open the Chicago Botanic Garden in 1972.

The garden, which is built on 9 different islands surrounded by lakes, takes up 155 hectares (385 acres) and is an important centre for learning and scientific research. It is made up of woods (100 acres), waterways (81 acres) and prairies (15 acres). And even though plants are the main focus, of course there are also birds (255 species!), butterflies, mammals, reptiles and amphibians. Some of the coolest gardens are the Japanese Garden, the Bonsai Collection, the Waterfall Garden and, of course, the Model Railroad Garden, where you can see landmarks from all over the country without ever leaving the city! The garden offers classes and summer camp sessions with hands-on science, gardening, art, nature and outdoor exploration. You can also stop by one evening for Nature Nights, a unique experience that allows families to discover the mysteries of nature at night!

cool, yEaH?

The garden is the home to over 2.3 million plants representing 9,434 plant varieties!

Every landmark in the Model Railroad Garden is made from natural materials including tree bark, seeds, acorns, twigs, stems, nuts, and other tree parts.

cool, yEaH?

Kenosha used to be called Masu-kinoja, which means 'trout come all at same time' in the Ojibwa language. Today's residents just call it K-Town or Keno.

Despite their small size, several of Kenosha's museums have been affiliated to the reputed Smithsonian Museum in Washington, D.C. since 2008!

last stop: KENOSHA

Get away to cottage country! You can avoid traffic jams by taking the train upstate to Waukegan and Kenosha from Chicago, or you can perhaps convince your parents to drive along the coast of Lake Michigan all the way to Kenosha. This way, you can stop at the little towns along the way, go for a swim or an icecream and watch a sunset on the lake.

Waukegan was one of the first settlements in Illinois. It used to be a French outpost and Potawatomi native settlement known as Little Fort. In 1829 the Potawamis signed a treaty giving their land to the Federal Government. By 1849 Little Fort was the county's capital, and the town decided to change its name to Waukegan (which means 'fort' or 'trading post' in the Potawami language). From then Waukegan grew as a port city for the Great Lakes. The old harbour and the white sand beach are still the best reasons to stop by.

If you continue upstate and cross the state border to Wisconsin, you'll arrive in Kenosha, Chicago's northernmost suburb. The Kenosha area was settled in prehistoric times by late Paleolitic Indians, about 13,500 years ago! There are lots of archaeological remnants around the city, with 23 historic landmarks and several museums to prove it: the Kenosha Public Museum, the Civil War Museum and the Dinosaur Discovery Museum. But best of all is Kenosha's historic streetcar system, which uses only vintage streetcars from all over the US, in different colours and with very distinct feel. They connect the coastal Harborpark to the city centre and the Metra trains to Chicago. There's no cooler ride along the amazing beach front!

HiKE, biKE oR paddlE youR caNoE

Chicago was a transportation hub long before trains arrived and made it a railway hub for the whole region. In 1848, the Illinois & Michigan Canal was built so that ships could travel from the Great Lakes to the Mississippi River and on to the Gulf of Mexico. It went all the way from the Bridgeport neighbourhood on the Chicago River to the town of LaSalle, Illinois, on the Illinois River. Because the Illinois River and Lake Michigan were at different heights—a 45m (140 foot) difference—17 locks were built along the new canal that connected them. A railroad was later built that ran parallel to the canal. The canal was used until 1933 for transporting goods and passengers, until trains became more common. In 1900, the Illinois & Michigan Canal was replaced by the Chicago Sanitary and Ship Canal, a much larger dig.

Big sections of the canal have been covered now, since it's not used anymore. What's left is a national heritage corridor made up of a park, hiking and biking trails, and a few museums and historical buildings. You can even canoe in the same canal once used by great cargo ships.

cool, yEaH?

The canal once ran 156 km (97 miles) from the Chicago River to the Illinois River.

When the flow of the Chicago River was reversed by engineers, all of the city's sewage was channelled through the canal! Yuck. (Nowadays, scientists think the river flows both ways, one direction on the surface, one at the bottom!).

a villagE WHERE timE stands still

Get ready to travel back in time. Waaaaaay back. We're talking before cell phones or digital cameras... before video games, iPods or even TV! Yup, that way back.

When you visit Naper Settlement, you'll step straight into a 19th century community. You'll meet costumed 'villagers' and walk through historic buildings as you learn about daily life in this time period. You'll visit the blacksmith's shop, stop by the stone carver's, go to school (like you really want to do that on your vacation!) and go get groceries.

As you wander around, you'll learn about the town's history and see its print shop, chapel and hotel. You'll also learn about how the availability of stone in the area, particularly after the Great Chicago Fire, was a boost for the economy of the town, since non-flammable building materials were in such high demand. It's a great way to go back to Chicago's roots, and learn where the city comes from in a fun way!

cool, yEaH?

This open-air museum has 30 historic buildings, 18 of which were relocated to the settlement.

In Naper's Copenhagen Schoolhouse, you can see real graffiti carved by schoolchildren way back in the 1840s. It just goes to show, some things never change!

113

COME RiDE tHE RaiLS

Chicago's central location made it the most important railroad centre in North America. The first locomotive to operate in Chicago left the city for the first time in 1848 on the Galena & Chicago Union railroad. It wasn't long before other railroads were built in and around the city. These connected Chicago with other major US cities and allowed for the transportation of food, livestock and other goods. It's no surprise that Chicago also became a major centre for the manufacture of trains. To this day, Chicago is a hub for rail travel. Trains allowed the city to expand and are still used to transport goods, and by those who live outside the city and need to come to Chicago.

The Illinois Railway Museum is the biggest railway museum in the US. It's a great place to learn about the history of the railroad and its role in Chicago's growth. There's a working streetcar line around the grounds that visitors can take to get from one barn to another. Each barn displays different types of trains and also artifacts like signs, tools, uniforms and buildings. But be careful when you hop on and off and when you're crossing the tracks!

You can also stop by the Fox River Trolley Museum. Visitors take an old-fashioned trolley car on a six-kilometre (four-mile) trip along Fox River and the Jon J. Duerr Forest Preserve. Many of the trolleys at the museum can still be ridden today.

cool, yEah?

The Illinois Railway Museum has two trains built for export to Russia during World Wars I and II. Neither one was ever delivered.

Feel like train watching? The Railway Museum's website (www.irm.org) has a real-time webcam where you can watch trains pull in and out of the station.

How Many thRills caN you pack iNto oNE SiNGlE day?

Six Flags Great America is a huge amusement park just outside Chicago. It is divided into different themed areas and includes a water park called Hurricane Harbor. There's something for everyone at Six Flags, with over 50 rides, including 13 scream-worthy roller coasters. Start your day by hopping on the Great America Scenic Railway and doing a circuit of the park so you can make a list of everything you plan to see! (You might as well arrive early to take advantage of your ticket and avoid the crowds).

Be a superhero for the day—feel what it's like to fly on Superman: Ultimate Flight. Or be saved by one—get caught up in Gotham City as it is torn apart by The Joker and then be saved by Batman, The Dark Knight.

And don't forget to stop by one of the shows to meet other members of the 'Justice League.' If cartoons are more your thing, visit Camp Cartoon, which has its very own roller coaster for kids—Spacely's Sprocket Rockets. And if you want to be in control, check out Winner's Circle Go carts and race your family and friends.

cool, yEaH?

Rue Le Dodge is the world's biggest bumper car floor.

The movie 'The Dark Knight' was mostly filmed on location in Chicago and was the base for one of the rides in Six Flags.

EAGLE

117

cool, yEah?

Skokie Park's Exploritorium has a playground made up of two-and-a-half-storey-tall tubes and tunnels!

The park district offers a ton of different summer camps. You can choose from a chess camp, circus camp, Broadway drama camp, urban adventure camp, soccer camp, and the list goes on...

play all day loNG iN tHis fuN-fillEd paRK distRict

Skokie Park District is not just an area full of parks, but there are indeed a lot of them—49 to be exact! You'll find it just north of downtown Chicago. The parks are all over the village, and accommodate baseball, softball, football and soccer fields; tennis, basketball and volleyball courts; and playgrounds.

The district is also home to cultural centres, a playhouse, an indoor playground, a water park, an ice rink and more! Take a golf lesson and then head over to the miniature golf course. Its theme is 'Around the World.' Putt under the Eiffel Tower, around a giant African elephant, through a Japanese garden or a waterfall on Easter Island and around the Great Wall of China. Who said geography couldn't be fun? Throughout the year the parks hold different events, and during the summer they offer different themed camps.

don't miss out on the mississippi

The Quad Cities is a metropolitan area on the state border between Illinois and Iowa, west of Chicago. It includes the cities of Davenport (Iowa), Moline (Illinois), Rock Island (Illinois), Bettendorf (Iowa) and East Moline (Illinois). Originally, the area was known as the "Tri-Cities" and only included Davenport, Rock Island and Moline. As the populations of cities in the area grew, East Moline was added, forming the Quad Cities. Eventually Bettendorf joined in too. The cities are located on both sides of the famous Mississippi River, the second longest river in the US, and one of the longest in the world. You might have heard about the Mississippi from the *Adventures of Tom Sawyer* and *Huckleberry Finn* by Mark Twain. And even though it is quite a drive from Chicago, it is totally worth it to at least set your eyes in one of the mightiest rivers on earth. You can even have your own little adventure by experiencing the Mississippi on a proper riverboat (you know, like those you remember from Tom Sawyer...). Some of the traditional Mississippi steamboats still serve as tour boats (although not on steam).

But the river isn't the only thing to see in the Quad Cities. You can ferry yourself from one to the next to feel the different atmospheres, and then just take advantage of all the activities in this metro area: mini-golf, water parks, bike trails, horseback riding, laser tag, go-carts, river cruises and plenty of festivals. It's definitely worth the drive. Besides, when will you ever be so close to this mythical river again?

cool, yEaH?

The name Quint Cities was proposed after Bettendorf became a 'Quad City,' but it never caught on, even though there are now five, not four, cities.

Even though the Mississippi is a north-south river, it flows east-west through the heart of the Quad Cities.

121

Adler Planetarium & Astronomy Museum
1300 S Lake Shore Dr, Chicago, IL 60605-2403. Bus: 146 to
Museum Campus. 312.922.STAR, www.adlerplanetarium.org. Hours:
Daily 9:30-4:30, First Fri of month to 10pm. Summer Hours: Daily
9:30-6pm, First Fri of month to 10pm Adults $10, Children (3-14) $6
*Shows and Audio Tour are extra.

American Girl Place
835 N Michigan Ave, Chicago, IL 60611. CTA L: Chicago (Red).
1.877.247.5223, www.americangirl.com. Hours: Mon-Thurs 10am-
9pm; Fri-Sat 9am-9pm; Sun 9am-7pm *Check website for seasonal
hours and Café hours.

Architecture Boat Tours
Several companies offer tours. Check their websites for tour types
and information.

(1) Chicago Architecture Foundation
312.922.3432, www.architecture.org. *All passengers boarding
vessels for the CAF architecture river cruise (and their carry-on items)
are subject to inspection pursuant to U.S. Coast Guard/Department of
Homeland Security regulations.

(2) Chicago History Museum
312.527.2002, www.chicagoline.com

(3) ShoreLine Sightseeing
312.222.9328, www.shorelinesightseeing.com

(4) Wendella Boats
312.337.1446, www.wendellaboats.com

(5) Seadog
www.seadogcruises.com/chicago/

Arlington Park
2200 W. Euclid, Arlington Heights, IL 60006. Metra: Arlington
847.385.7500, www.arlingtonpark.com. Adults $7, Seniors $3,
Children (under 17) Free. *Check website for hours and events

Art Institute of Chicago
111 South Michigan Ave, Chicago, IL 60603. CTA L: Adams/Wabash,
Metra: Van Buren. 312.443.3600, www.artic.edu. Hours: Mon-Fri
10:30am-5pm (Thurs to 8pm); Sat-Sun 10am-5pm. Adults $12,
Seniors $7, Children (under 12) Free.

Blue Man Group
Briar Street Theatre, 3133 N Halsted, Chicago, IL 60657. CTA L:
Belmont. 773.348.4000, www.blueman.com. Tickets $49-$64 *Check
website for showtimes, tickets, student pricing and special offers.

Buckingham Fountain & Grant Park
Columbus Dr & Congress Pkwy, Chicago, IL. CTA L: Library or
Harrison. www.cpdit01.com/resources/buckingham_fountain.cfm.
Hours: Park: Daily. Fountain: Daily Apr to mid-Oct 8am-11pm. Free.

Chicago Architecture Foundation
224 S Michigan Ave, Chicago, IL 60604. CTA L: Adams/Wabash

312.922.3432, www.architecture.org. *Check website for information on tours, exhibits, programs and shop.

Chicago Botanic Garden
1000 Lake Cook Rd, Glencoe, IL 60022. Metra: Glencoe (for Trolley to Garden) or Braeside. 847.835.5440, www.chicago-botanic.org Hours: Garden: Daily 8am-sunset.Buildings close at different times; check website. Free.

Chicago History Museum
1601 N Clark St, Chicago, IL 60614-6038. CTA: Sedgwick or Clark/Division. Bus: 11, 22, 36, 72, 73, 151, 156. Tel. 312.642.4600, www.chicagohistory.org. Hours: Mon-Sat 9:30-4:30 (Thurs to 8:00) Sun 12pm-5pm. Adults $14, Seniors & Students (13-22) $12, Children (12 and under) Free – Includes Audio Tour. Mondays Free.

Chicago International Children's Film Festival
Facets Multi-Media, Inc.
1517 West Fullerton Ave, Chicago, IL 60614. 773.281.9075, www.cicff.org. *Check website for current events and times

DuSable Museum of African American History
740 E 56th Place, Chicago, IL 60637. Metra: 55th-56th-57th 773.947.0600, www.dusablemuseum.org. Hours: Tues-Sat 10am-5pm, Sun noon-5pm. Adults $3, Seniors $2, Students $2, Children (6-13) $1, Children (under 6) Free. Sundays Free.

Ernest Hemingway Birthplace & Museum
200 N Oak Park Ave, Oak Park, IL 60302. CTA L: Oak Park Avenue Birthplace 708.445.3071 Museum 708.524.5383, www.ehfop.org. Hours: Sun-Fri 1pm-5pm. Sat 10am-5pm. Adults $8, Seniors $6, Youth (under 18) $6, Children (under 5) Free

Field Museum
1400 S Lake Shore Dr, Chicago, IL 60605. CTA L: Roosevelt. Metra: Roosevelt Road. 312.922.9410, www.fieldmuseum.org. Hours: Daily 9am-5pm. Adults $22, Seniors $19, Students $19, Children (4-11) $12.

Flying Gaonas Gym
773.398.9881, www.flyinggaonastrapeze.com
*The school moves, so make sure to check out the website for its current location. Make sure you wear comfortable clothing that allows for movement.

Frank Lloyd Wright Home & Studio
951 Chicago Ave, Oak Park, IL. CTA L: Oak Park Avenue 708.848.1976, www.wrightplus.org/homestudio/homestudio.html Hours: Mon-Wed, Fri 11am, 1pm, 3pm. Wed (May-Aug) 11am, 1pm, 3pm, 4pm, 5pm, 6pm. Sat-Sun 11am-3:30pm (tours every 20 minutes). Adults $12, Seniors $10, Youth (11-18) $10, Children (4-10) $5 *Design Detectives Family Tour - Saturdays only.
Bring your family of sleuths together and explore Wright's home to uncover the secrets of his designs. Join Preservation Trust Junior

Interpreters, specially trained 5th-10th grade students, to discover how America's most famous architect broke with traditional design, and hear stories of his family's life in his Oak Park house.

Garfield Park Conservatory
300 N Central Park Ave, Chicago, IL 60624. CTA L: Conservatory-Central Park Drive. 312.746.5100, www.garfield-conservatory.org
Hours: Daily 9am-5pm (Thurs until 8pm). Free.

Graceland Cemetery
4001 N Clark St, Chicago, IL 60613. CTA L: Sheridan. 773.525.1105
www.gracelandcemetery.org. Hours: Daily 8am-4:30pm. Free.

Illinois & Michigan Canal
www.nps.gov/ilmidnr.state.il.us/lands/LANDMGT/PARKS/I&M/Main.htm.

Jay Pritzker Pavilion
See Millennium Park. *Check website for current events. Grant Park Music Festival: www.grantparkmusicfestival.com.

Jazz & Blues
Dearborn Station.
47 W Polk St, Chicago, IL 60605. 312.360.0234,
www.jazzshowcase.com. Hours: Mon-Sat 8pm & 10pm
Sun 4pm*, 8pm & 10pm. * Sun 4pm is geared toward children.

Joe's Be-Bop Café and Jazz Emporium
700 E Grand Ave, Chicago, IL 60611. 312.595.JAZZ, www.joesbebop.com. Hours: Sun-Thurs 11am-8pm. Fri-Sat 11am-10pm.
*Jazz Showcase moves between clubs (it has no permanent location) so make sure you check out the website before heading over.
**The Chicago Office of Tourism offers the Chicago Blues Audio Tour, narrated by Buddy Guy and highlights blues' history and its effect on popular music and American culture.

House of Blues
329 N Dearborn, Chicago, IL 60654, 312.923.2000
www.hob.com/chicago.

Blue Chicago
736 N Clark, Chicago, IL 60610, 312.642.6261
536 N Clark, Chicago, IL 60610, 312.661.0100
www.bluechicago.com

John Hancock Center & Observatory
875 N Michigan Ave, Chicago, IL 60611. CTA L: Chicago (Red)
312.751.3681, 1.888.875.VIEW (8439), www.hancockobservatory.com. Hours: Daily 9am-11pm. Adults $15, Seniors $13, Children (5-12) $9.

Lake & River Cruises
See Architecture Boat Tours.

Lakefront & Beach
www.chicagoparkdistrict.com

Lincoln Park Zoo
2001 N Clark St, Chicago, IL 60614. Bus: 151 or 156.
312.742.2000, www.lpzoo.org. Hours: Grounds: Daily 9am-6pm
Buildings & Farm: Daily 10am-5pm. *Check website for winter and
summer hours. Free.

Magnificent Mile
The Greater North Michigan Avenue Association, 625 North Michigan
Avenue, Suite 401, Chicago, IL 60611. CTA L: Grand or Chicago
(Red). 312.642.3570. Seasonal Event Hotline: 312.409.5560
www.themagnificentmile.com

McCormick Tribune Ice Rink
See Millennium Park

Millennium Park
Michigan Ave & Randolph St. CTA L: Lake or Randolph.
Metra: Millennium. 312.742.1168, www.millenniumpark.org
Hours: Mon-Sun 6am-11pm. Free.
Check the website prior to your visit for activities and exhibitions.

Mitchell Museum of the American Indian
3001 Central St, Evanston, IL 60201. CTA L: Central Street (then bus
201), Metra: Central Street (then bus 201). 847.475.1030, www.
mitchellmuseum.org. Hours: Tues-Sat 10am-5pm (Thurs until 8pm).
Suggested admission: Adults $5, Seniors $2.50, Students $2.50,
Children $2.50, Family $10.

Money Museum
230 LaSalle St, Chicago, IL. CTA L: Quincy. 312.322.2400, www.
chicagofed.org/education/money_museum.cfm. Hours: Mon-Fri 9am-
4pm (closed Bank Holidays). Free. Note: As a federal facility, photo
identification is required, and personal and/or bag searches may be
required prior to admittance.

Museum of Contemporary Art
220 East Chicago Ave, Chicago, IL 60611, CTA L: Chicago (Red)
312.280.2660, www.mcachicago.org. Hours: Tues-Sun 10am-5pm
(Tues until 8pm). Adults $10, Seniors $6, Students $6, Children
(under 12) Free. *Free daily tours are available – check website for
schedule

Museum of Science and Industry
57th Street and Lake Shore Drive, Chicago, IL 60637. Metra: 57th
Street. 773.684.1414, www.msichicago.org. Hours: Mon-Thurs
9:30am-4pm
Fri-Sat 9:30am-5:30pm. Sun 11am-5:30pm. Adults $13, Seniors $12,
Children (3-11) $9. *Some exhibits may have additional charges.

Naper Settlement
523 South Webster St, Naperville, IL 60540. Metra: Naperville (1 mile
from Settlement). 630.420.6010, www.napersettlement.org. Hours:
Apr-Oct: Tues-Sat 10am-4pm; Sun 1pm-4pm. Nov-Mar: Mon-Fri
10am-4pm. Adults $8, Seniors $7, Youth (4-17) $5.50 (Apr-Oct).

Adults $4.25, Seniors $3.75, Youth (4-17) $3 (Nov-Mar).

National Museum of Mexican Art

1852 W 19th St, Chicago, IL 60608. CTA L: 18th Street.
312.738.1503, www.nationalmuseumofmexicanart.org. Hours: Tues-Sun 10am-5pm. Free. *Events may have additional charges.

Navy Pier

600 East Grand Ave, Chicago, IL 60611. CTA L: Grand (Red).
312.595.PIER (7437); 1.800.595.PIER (7437), www.navypier.com.

Neighborhood Tours

77 E Randolph St, Chicago, IL. 312.742.1190, www.
ChicagoNeighborhoodTours.com. Hours: See website for tour
schedules. Adults $30, Seniors/Students/Children (8-18) $25. *Local
residents take visitors into these unique neighbourhoods, including
Historic Bronzeville, Little Italy, Pilsen & Little Village, Pullman Historic
District, Wicker Park & Bucktown.

Noble Horse Theatre

1410 N Orleans St, Chicago, IL 60610. CTA L: Sedgwick.
312.266.7878, www.noblehorsechicago.com. Hours: Box office:
Mon-Fri 9am-6pm. Magnificent Mile Carriages: Daily 10am-4:30pm;
6pm-midnight. *Check website for showtimes.

O'Leary's Chicago Fire Truck Tours

Michigan Ave & Illinois St. CTA L: Grand (Red). 312.287.6565
www.olearysfiretours.com, www.chicagofiretrucktour.com. Hours:
Seasonal – call for tour times. Adults $20, Seniors $10, Children
(under 12) $10. *A tour in one of these vintage fire trucks will show
you the city from a unique perspective, and it's a great way to learn
more about the Great Chicago Fire and to visit authentic Chicago fire
stations.

Oriental Institute Museum

1155 East 58th St, Chicago, IL 60637. Metra: 59th Street.
773.702.9520, oi.uchicago.edu/museum/. Hours: Tues-Sat 10am-6pm
(Wed until 8:30pm). Sun noon-6pm. Free. Suggested donation: Adults
$5, Children (under 12) $2.

Peggy Notebaert Nature Museum

2430 N Cannon Dr, Chicago, IL 60614. Bus: 151 or 156 to Fullerton
Pkwy/Stockton Dr; 77. 773.755.5100. www.chias.org. Hours: Mon-Fri
9am-4:30pm. Sat-Sun 10am-5pm. Adults $9, Seniors $7, Students $7,
Children 3-12 $6, Children (under 3) Free. *Thurs suggested donation

Polish Museum of America

984 N. Milwaukee Ave, Chicago, IL 60642. CTA L: Chicago (Blue)
773.384.3352, www.polishmuseumofamerica.org. Hours: Fri-Wed
11am-4pm. Suggested donation: Adults $5, Seniors $4, Students $4,
Children (under 12) $3.

Quad Cities

www.quadcities.com, www.visitquadcities.com.

Railway Museums

Fox River Trolley Museum
361 South LaFox St (Illinois Route 31), South Elgin, IL 60177. Metra: Elgin (then bus 801 to State St). 847.697.4676, www.foxtrolley.org. Hours: Seasonal – check website. All-Day Ticket $7.

Illinois Railway Museum
7000 Olson Rd, Union, IL 60180. 815.923.4000; 1.800.BIG.RAIL (244.7245), www.irm.org. Hours: Seasonal – check website. Adults $8-$12, Children $4-$8, Family $25-$45.

Robie House
5757 S Woodlawn Ave, Chicago, IL 60637. Metra: 59th Street. 708.848.1976, www.gowright.org/robiehouse/robiehouse.html. Tour Hours: Sat 11am-3pm (November 1, 2008 – October 31, 2009).Adults $12, Seniors $10, Youth (11-18) $10, Children (4-10) $5.

Sculpture Tour
Chicago Cultural Center, 78 E. Washington St., Chicago, IL 60602. 312.742.1164, egov.cityofchicago.org/publicart. *Pick up a guide at the Chicago Cultural Center.

Sears Tower Skydeck
233 S Wacker Dr, Chicago, IL 60606. CTA L: Quincy. 312.875.9447, www.the-skydeck.com. Hours: Apr-Sept Daily 10am-10pm. Oct-Mar Daily 10am-8pm. Adults $12.95, Youth (3-11) $9.50, Children (under 3) Free. *Skylights Audio Tour extra; Enter Skydeck on Jackson Blvd

Shedd Aquarium
1200 S Lake Shore Dr, Chicago, IL 60605. CTA L: Roosevelt. Metra: Roosevelt Road. 312.939.2438, www.sheddaquarium.org. Hours: Mon-Fri 9am-5pm. Sat-Sun 9am-6pm. Adults $17.95, Seniors $13.95, Children (3-11) $13.95

Six Flags Great America
1 Great America Parkway, Gurnee, IL 60031. Metra: Waukegan or Libertyville (then bus 572). 847.249.INFO (4636), 847.249.2133, www.sixflags.com/greatamerica. Hours: Seasonal – check website. Adults $54.99, Children (under 48 inches tall) $34.99, Children (2 and under) Free.

Skokie Park District
9300 Weber Park Place. Skokie, IL 60077. 847.674.1500. www.skokieparkdistrict.org. Hours: Facility Specific – refer to website. *See website for locations and rates of specific facilities.

Spertus Institute
610 S Michigan Ave, Chicago, IL 60605. CTA L: Harrison. 312.322.1700, www.spertus.edu. Hours: Sun-Thurs 10am-5pm (Thurs until 6pm). Fri 10am-3pm. Adults $7, Seniors $5, Students $5, Children (under 5) Free. *Free Tues 10am-noon & Thurs 2pm-6pm.

Swedish American Museum Center
5211 N. Clark St, Chicago, IL 60640. CTA L: Berwyn. 773.728.8111,

www.samac.org. Hours: Tues-Fri 10am-4pm. Sat-Sun 11am-4pm
Children's Museum 1pm-4pm. Adults $4, Seniors $3, Students $3,
Children $3, Family $10. Free second Tues of every month; Check
website for holiday hours.

Unity Temple
875 Lake St, Oak Park, IL 60301. CTA L: Oak Park Avenue.
708.383.8873, www.utrf.org. Hours: Mon-Fri 10:30am-4:30pm. Sat-
Sun 1pm-4pm. Adults $8, Seniors $6, Students (6-22) $6.

Untouchable Tours
Clark St & Ohio Ave, Chicago, IL. CTA L: Grand (Red). 773.881.1195,
www.gangstertour.com. Hours: Seasonal – check website for tour
times. Adults $27.

Water Parks
CoCo Key Water Resorts
Sheraton Chicago Northwest, 3400 W Euclid Ave, Arlington Heights,
IL 60005. 847.394.2000, www.cocokeywaterresort.com. Hours: Sea-
sonal – check website. Day Passes: Fri-Sun $39, Mon-Thurs $25
*Day Passes are subject to availability based on waterpark capacity

Mayan Adventure Indoor Waterpark
Holiday Inn Chicago-Elmhurst, 624 North York Rd, Elmhurst, IL
60126. 630.279.1100; 1.877.H2O.4FUN (426.4356), www.mayan-
indoorwaterpark.com. Hours: Seasonal – check website. Half Day
Passes $20, Full Day Pass $30. *Day Passes are subject to availability based on waterpark capacity.

Pelican Harbor Indoor/Outdoor Aquatic Park
Bolingbrook Recreation & Aquatic Complex, 200 S. Lindsey Lane
(630) 739-1705, www.bolingbrookparks.org/facilities/pelicanharbor.
Hours: Mon, Wed, Fri 4pm-8pm. Sat noon-8pm. Sun noon-6pm.
Adults $8, Children $8, Children (under 2) Free.

cHild-FRiENdly HotEl pick

Hilton Suites Chicago Magnificent Mile
198 E Delaware Place, Chicago, IL 60611. Tel. 312.664.1100.
www.chicagomagnificentmile.hilton.com. The Hilton is located
right across the road from the
John Hancock Center, the famous
Cheese Cake Factory, Chicago
Water Tower, the Magnificent Mile
and the Museum of Contemporary
Art. Family suites, an indoors
swimming pool and a kid-friendly
rapport make it our top pick in town.

RECommENdEd HotEl

Chicago's Essex Inn
800 S Michigan Ave, Chicago,
IL 60605. 312.939.2800
Reservations 1.800.621.6909,
www.essexinn.com
Across the road from Grant
Park, just south of the Loop.
Easy access. Millennium Park's
doorstep. Great lake views.

Wrigley Field
1060 W Addison St, Chicago, IL 60613. CTA L: Addison. 773.404.
CUBS (2827), chicago.cubs.mlb.com/chc/ballpark/index.jsp
*Check website for tour and Cubs game information

RESTAURANTS

Ed Debevic's
640 N Wells St, Chicago, IL 60620. 312.664.1707,
www.eddebevics.com. A 1950's style diner with extremely talkative
and wisecracking wait staff.

ESPN Zone
43 E Ohio St, Chicago, IL 60611. 312.644.3776, www.espnzone.
com/chicago. A sports-themed restaurant with a huge screen.

Garrett Popcorn Shops
26 West Randolph, Chicago, IL 60601; 4 East Madison, Chicago,
IL 60602; 2 West Jackson, Chicago, IL 60604; 500 W Madison St -
CitiCorp Center - 2nd Flr, Chicago, IL 60661. A selection of flavoured
popcorn. It's very popular, so don't be surprised if you need to line up.

Hard Rock Cafe Chicago
63 W Ontario St, Chicago, IL 60610. 312.943.2252.
www.hardrock.com/chicago. Rock'n'Roll and music theme.

McDonald's 50th Anniversary Restaurant
600 N Clark St, Chicago, IL 60654. 312.867.0455. www.mcdonalds.
com. A one-of-a-kind futuristic McDonald's.

Rainforest Café
605 N Clark St, Chicago, IL 60654. 312.787.1501. www.rainforestca-
fe.com. A themed restaurant with a jungle setting features animated
animals and live fish.

Taste of Chicago
Grant Park, 300 S Columbus Dr, Chicago IL 60604. 312.744.3315.
www.tasteofchicago.us. A 10-day annual event with over 300 menu
items from over 70 restaurants.

Photograph credits and copyrights (clockwise from top left):

Cover Art: Tapan Gandhi (logo); David Finkelstein (drawing); Kim Sokol (stamp); A.J. Palmer (font). **Characters:** Mike Hiscott. **All stamps:** Kim Sokol. **Front cover endpaper:** courtesy City of Chicago. 1: logo courtesy asm; stamp Kim sokol. 3: asm students. 6: National Atlas of the United States/US Dept. Interior. 7: City of Chicago. 8: City of Chicago (logo). 9-11: all sw/jj. 12-13: pfm/jj. 14-15: courtesy City of Chicago/Peter J. Schulz. Top-5 16-17: Inuksuk by Peter Irniq, artwork photo courtesy The Field Museum /w/cc-sa-2.5 (cropped); Valérie75 /w/cc-by-sa-2.5; courtesy The Field Museum; courtesy The Field Museum. 18-19: sw/jj; pfm/jj (cropped); James Keenan Poole /wc/gnu-fdl-1.2; sw/jj. 20-21: courtesy Millennium Park/City of Chicago; pfm/jj; courtesy Millennium Park/City of Chicago; sw/jj; courtesy Millennium Park/City of Chicago; courtesy Millennium Park/City of Chicago. 22: all pfm/jj. 23: sw/jj (cropped). 24-25: all courtesy Shedd Aquarium. Attractions 26-27: all sw/jj. 29: all pfm/jj. 30-31: pfm/jj; pd. 32-33: courtesy Chicago Architecture Foundation (CAF); Anne Evans, courtesy CAF; pfm/jj; pfm/jj; pfm/jj. 34-35: sw/jj; sw/jj; sw/jj; pd. 37: sw/jj; Padraic Ryan /w/gnu-fdl-1.2 or cc-by-sa-3.0; pd; pd; pd.38-39: Al Ravenna /wc/pd; wc/pd; sw/jj. 40: sw/jj; AudeVivere /w/cc-by-sa-2.5. 42-43: all sw/jj. 44-45: Payton Chung /w/cc-by-2.0; sw/jj; sw/jj; Jeremy Atherton w/cc-by-sa-2.5; sw/jj. 47: sw/jj; courtesy City of Chicago/Chris McGuire; courtesy City of Chicago/Peter J. Schulz. 48-49: courtesy Lincoln Park Zoo; courtesy Lincoln Park Zoo; sw/jj; courtesy Lincoln Park Zoo; courtesy Lincoln Park Zoo. 50: sw/jj; sw/jj; courtesy Money Museum; sw/jj. 52-53: sw/jj; sw/jj; Kabies /w/cc-by-2.0. 54-55: all sw/jj. 56-57: all sw/jj. 58: all sw/jj. 60-61: courtesy Smart Destinations Inc. (GoChicago Card); sw/jj; courtesy Peggy Notebaert Nature Museum; sw/jj. 62-63: pfm/jj; Lykantrop /w; pd; sw/jj. 64-65: wc/gnu-fdl-1.2; Daniel Schwen /w/gnu-fdl-1.2; DeansFA /wc/gnu-fdl-1.2; Jaro Nemcok /w/cc-by-sa-3.0. 66-67: William Zbaren, courtesy Spertus Institute of Jewish Studies; Dawn E. Roscoe, courtesy Spertus Institute of Jewish Studies; Dawn E. Roscoe, courtesy Spertus Institute of Jewish Studies; Dawn E. Roscoe, courtesy Spertus Institute of Jewish Studies; sw/jj. 68: all sw/jj. Activities 72-73: all sw/jj. 74: David Hawe, courtesy Blue Man Productions, Inc. 76-77: pfm/jj; Anne Evans, courtesy Chicago Architecture Foundation (CAF); Anne Evans, courtesy CAF. 78: all courtesy Facets Multi-Media Inc. (except popcorn, ricardo / zone41.net cc-by-sa-2.0; popcorn bag Sapo.pt). 81: all courtesy Flying Gaonas. 82-83: all pd. 84-85: Matthias Beiling; courtesy City of Chicago/Peter J. Schulz. 86-87: pfm/jj; Rickdrew /w/gnu-fdl-1.2 or cc-by-sa-2.5; pfm/jj. 88: Will Rossiter /pd; pd; New York World Telegram /pd. 90-91: courtesy The Greater North Michigan Avenue Association; courtesy The Greater North Michigan Avenue Association; pfm/jj; pfm/jj. 92: courtesy Millennium Park; courtesy Millennium Park; pfm/jj. 94-95: pfm/jj; sw/jj; pfm/jj; pfm/jj. 96: pd; courtesy Noble Horse Theatre; BLW /w/pd; Harry Pujols (Flickr) /cc-by-sa-2.0). 98-99: pfm/jj; sw/jj; pfm/jj. 100-101: all sw/jj. 102-103: courtesy CoCo Key Water Resort/Sheraton Chicago NW; SajorR /w/cc-by-sa-2.5; Solitude /w/gnu-fdl-1.2. Out-of-Town 104-105: courtesy Arlington Park Racetrack; pfm/jj. 106-107: all courtesy Chicago Botanic Garden. 108: /w/pd; Kenokewl /w/pd; Kenokewl /w/gnu-fdl-1.2. 110: pd. 111: all Illinoistocht/Jim /pd. 112-113: all courtesy Naper Settlement. 114-115: stamps/logos all pd; Sean Lamb /w/cc-by-sa-2.0; Sean Lamb /w/cc-by-sa-2.0; pd. 116: all courtesy Six Flags Great America. 118-119: courtesy Skokie Park District; courtesy Skokie Park District; courtesy Skokie Park District; Vytis /w/gnu-fdl-1.2. 120-121: all courtesy Quad Cities Convention Center. **Back cover end paper:** courtesy CTA.

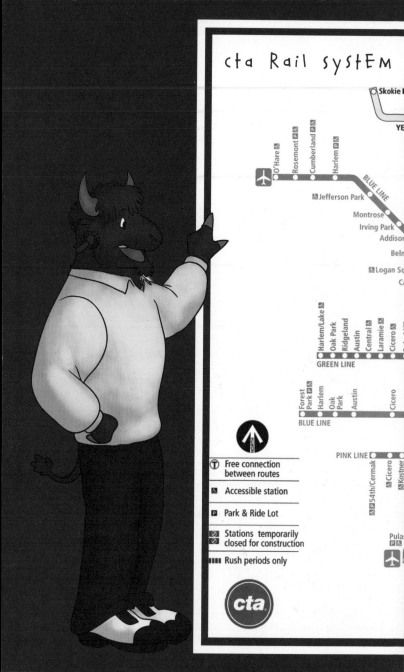

cta Rail systEm

Skokie

YE

O'Hare ✈
Rosemont P ♿
Cumberland P ♿
Harlem P ♿

BLUE LINE

♿ Jefferson Park

Montrose
Irving Park
Addison
Belm
♿ Logan Sq
Ca

Harlem/Lake ♿
Oak Park
Ridgeland
Austin
Central ♿
Laramie ♿
Cicero ♿

GREEN LINE

Forest Park P ♿
Harlem
Oak Park
Austin
Cicero

BLUE LINE

PINK LINE

54th/Cermak ♿ P
Cicero ♿
Kostner ♿

Pula
P ♿

✈ ♿

🔵 Free connection between routes

♿ Accessible station

P Park & Ride Lot

Stations temporarily closed for construction

IIII Rush periods only

cta